D1224781

Length

Julie Murray

Abdo Kids Junior
is an Imprint of Abdo Kids
abdobooks.com

Abdo
MEASURE IT!
Kids

abdobooks.com

Published by Abdo Kids, a division of ABDO, P.O. Box 398166, Minneapolis, Minnesota 55439.
Copyright © 2020 by Abdo Consulting Group, Inc. International copyrights reserved in all countries.
No part of this book may be reproduced in any form without written permission from the publisher.
Abdo Kids Junior™ is a trademark and logo of Abdo Kids.

Printed in the United States of America, North Mankato, Minnesota.

052019

092019

THIS BOOK CONTAINS
RECYCLED MATERIALS

Photo Credits: Alamy, iStock, Shutterstock

Production Contributors: Teddy Borth, Jennie Forsberg, Grace Hansen

Design Contributors: Christina Doffing, Candice Keimig, Dorothy Toth

Library of Congress Control Number: 2018963318

Publisher's Cataloging-in-Publication Data

Names: Murray, Julie, author.

Title: Length / by Julie Murray.

Description: Minneapolis, Minnesota : Abdo Kids, 2020 | Series: Measure it! |
    Includes online resources and index.

Identifiers: ISBN 9781532185281 (lib. bdg.) | ISBN 9781532186264 (ebook) |
    ISBN 9781532186752 (Read-to-me ebook)

Subjects: LCSH: Length measurement--Juvenile literature. | Size and shape--
    Juvenile literature. | Measurement--Juvenile literature.

Classification: DDC 530.813--dc23

Table of Contents

Length

Length tells us how long something is.

A ruler measures length. It is 12 inches (30.48 cm) long. That equals 1 foot.

How long is the top of the rocket? Dan measures. It is about 1 foot (.3 m).

9

The iguana is 6 feet (1.8 m) long!

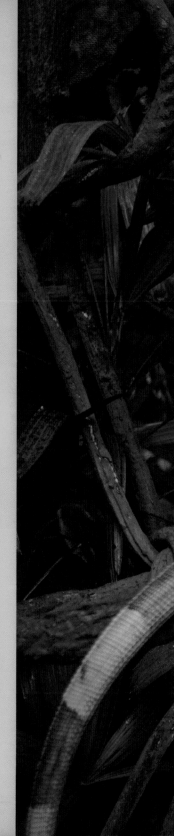

A ruler has centimeters too.

1 inch is equal to 2.54 cm.

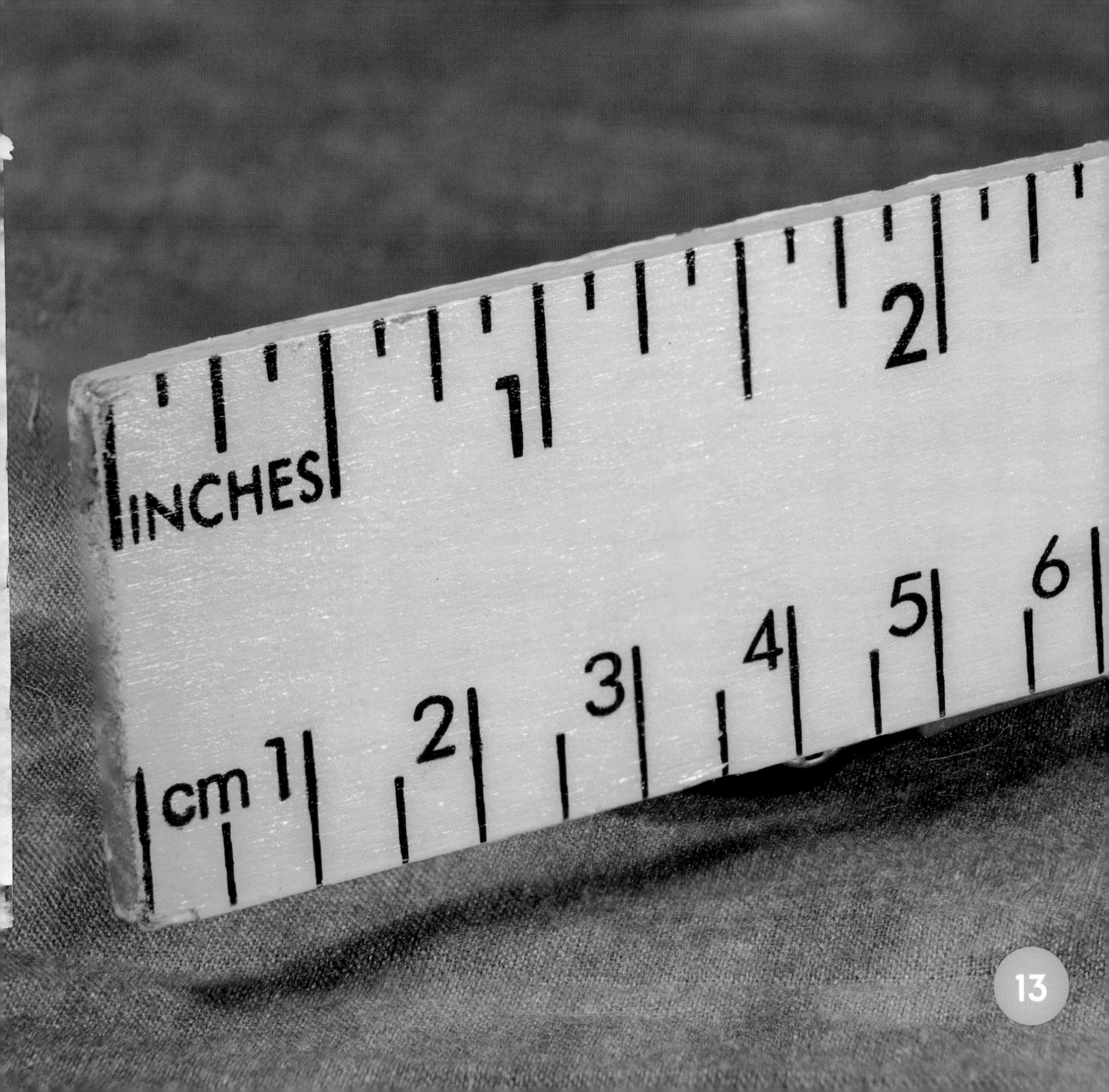
INCHES
1
2
cm 1
2
3
4
5
6

How long is a penny?

Gus measures. It is

2 cm (0.79 in) long.

A yard is 3 feet (91.44 cm) long.
A football field is 100 yards
(91.44 m).

17

One mile is 5,280 feet (1.61 km). Jay rides the bus 3 miles (4.83 km) to school.

How long is the shoe?

Let's Review!

What is the length of each item?

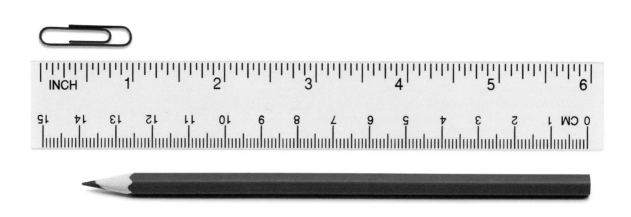

Glossary

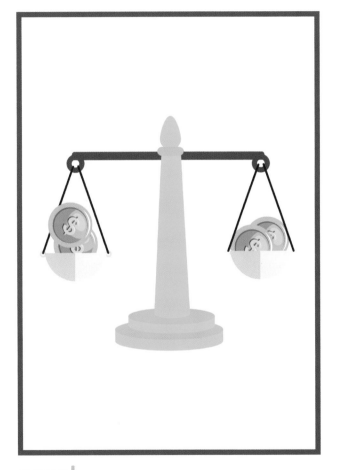

equal
a thing that has the same length
or amount as something else.

measure
to find the length or amount
of something.

Index

Abdo Kids
ONLINE
FREE! ONLINE MULTIMEDIA RESOURCES

Visit **abdokids.com**
to access crafts, games,
videos, and more!

Use Abdo Kids code
MLK5281
or scan this QR code!